Mike Pow[er]
PUB WAL[KS]
ALONG THE
DORSET COAST

Introduction

Dorset is probably the most scenic county in England but I'm probably biased – I was born here. The entire coastline measures some 76 miles in length. Starting a mile west from Lyme Regis it finishes at Highcliffe in the east. Vast areas of heath and grassland stretch towards sheltered bays, cut by the sea into the steep cliffs.   Geologically Dorset is of great importance commencing with the large white cliffs at Ballard which run continuously to Weymouth. Chesil Beach a vast shingle bank starts here finishing some 11 miles later beyond Abbotsbury. Continue westwards and we reach an area of constant landslips.

The army occupy a vast area stretching from Kimmeridge to Lulworth with access only possible at certain times. Purbeck and Portland are famous for their quarries the hard marble used extensively over the centuries in the construction industry whilst doted at intervals are the large holiday towns of Bournemouth, Poole, Swanage, Weymouth and Lyme Regis. Many people, including hundreds of walkers come here just for the sheer beauty, the peace and tranquillity. On a sunny summers' day I can think of no finer place to be.

I have chosen ten of my favourite pubs with an associated circular walk. They vary in length from 2 - $5\frac{1}{2}$ miles, are described in detail each with an accompanying sketch map. I always enjoy these walks I hope you will too.

© Power Publications
1 Clayford Ave
Ferndown
Dorset. BH22 9PQ

ISBN 1898073 21 X

Other local publications

Pub Walks in Dorset
40 More Pub Walks in Dorset
Pub Walks in Hardy's Wessex
The Dorset Coast Path
A Mountain Bike Guide to Dorset
Ancient Stones of Dorset
A Century of Cinema in Dorset

Publisher's note
Whilst every care has been taken to ensure that all the information contained in this book is correct neither the authors or publishers can accept any responsibility for any inaccuracies that may occur

Front cover: The Anchor Inn, Seatown. Back cover: Chapman's Pool

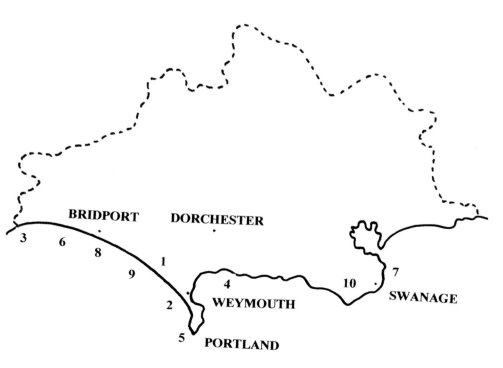

BRIDPORT   DORCHESTER

3   6

8

9   1

2   WEYMOUTH

10   7

SWANAGE

5   PORTLAND

4

Walk No. 1
The Swan Inn & Ilchester Arms, Abbotsbury

This lovely historic Dorset village lies on the B3157 between Weymouth and Bridport.

There are two pubs in the village, the Swan, sometimes open all day in the season and serving traditional English fayre and the more atmospheric 16th century Ilchester Arms. The inn has ten letting rooms and presently opens all day from 11–11. Children are welcome away from the bars. Park in the main car park next to the Swan.

Approximate distance: 2½ miles. OS maps: Landranger 194 and Outdoor Leisure 15. Reference 578/853.

Abbotsbury lies in a sheltered green valley its name derived from the large Benedictine abbey that was founded in the middle of the 11th century and destroyed by Henry VIII during the Reformation. The Tithe Barn, built around 1400 was originally twice its present size indicating the wealth of the abbey. The Children's Farm is open 7 days a week between 10 and 6 from Easter till October. Tel: (01305) 871817. No dogs. World famous Abbotsbury Gardens are open all year round. Covering an area of 20 acres the gardens were established in the 18th century as a kitchen garden to the Countess of Ilchester's castle that once overlooked Chesil Beach, part of the perimeter wall can still be seen. Tel: (01305) 871387. Abbotsbury Swannery is open every day from mid March till late October opening at 10 am with the last admission at 5 pm. From late March to the end of April hundreds of swans come together competing for nesting space Tel: (01305 871858).

This very interesting walk ideal for families, commences at St Nicholas's church then follows a track past Abbotsbury Gardens to the Chesil Beach, for the more energetic an optional path will take you up to St Catherine's Chapel. The route then guides you to the Swannery, up past the Tithe Barn and through the remains of the abbey. Although not too demanding the tracks can be wet and muddy during the winter months.

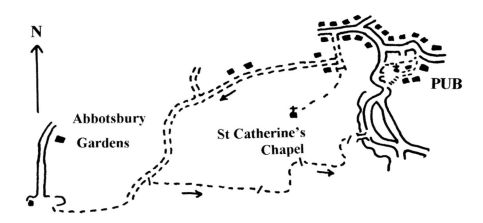

Cross the car park to St Nicholas church entering through the rear gate. It was built as the parish church alongside the abbey in the late 14th or early 15th century. Inside the porch is an effigy of one of the early abbots. Leave by the gate on the far side turning right into the lane and continue ahead, up and through the village past the Ilchester Arms walking until you reach Chapel Lane on the left. Go past the stores and up to the gate. (If you wish to visit the chapel follow the path ahead returning to the track west of the chapel. Dedicated to St Catherine, the patron saint of spinsters, it was built in the 15th century as part of the abbey. It is a vital mark for shipping). Continue down the track, past a few dwellings turning left at the cross track.

Carry on down until you reach the second stile on the left or keep straight ahead to reach the shingle bank and Abbotsbury Gardens situated a short way up the hill on the right. Back at the stile cross the field staying close to the fence from where you have lovely views of the Fleet. Keep to the path round then uphill until you reach the stile on the right. Continue beside the hedge up to the stile and out onto the track. Turn right to visit the Swannery otherwise go left up to meet the lane by the Tithe Barn.

Ten paces up the hill take the footpath on the right signposted, Village Car Park & St Nicholas Church. The gable end is all that now remains from the once large abbey. Turn right by Abbey House Tea Rooms and GuestHouse returning to the car park

The Elm Tree, Langton Herring

Langton Herring is signed from the B3157 Chickerell to Portesham road.

Pub located next to the church. This well kept pub has several cosy rooms festooned with lots of bright shining copper and brass. There is an interesting menu available every day and a good choice of real ales. Children are welcome. Hours are all day 11–11 and 12–10.30 on Sunday. Walkers are welcome to park in the paddock at the side of the pub.

Approximate distance 2 miles: OS maps: Landranger 194 & Outdoor Leisure 15. Reference 615/825.

In Anglo-Saxon times the village was known as Langetone but after the manor was acquired by the Harang family it became Langton Herring. A short distance down the field on the north side of the approach road a well-preserved limekiln can be seen.

Ideal for all weather conditions this peaceful scenic walk is neither long nor over demanding making it ideal for all members of the family. In part it follows the Dorset Coast Path beside the Fleet, the largest lagoon in Britain. Originating in 1393 it is an outstanding nature reserve. Thousands of wildfowl can regularly be seen feeding on the eel grass. Chesil Beach, a vast shingle bank which protects the lagoon is approximately 29 kilometres in length and one of nature's wonders formed naturally at the end of the last ice age. It provides a perfect nesting site for the little tern. During the last war Sir Barnes Wallis used the area to test his bouncing bombs before they were deployed in the destruction of the Moehne and Eder Dams.

Leave the car park turning right then go right again behind the pub, down and round the charming little church of St Peter. At the end of the village turn left onto the bridleway, walk up to the bend and climb the step stone stile beside the gate. Immediately turn right crossing the stile into the field. Bearing half-left follow the well beaten path across to the stone stile on the far side and turn left to rejoin the track.

Carry on down towards the Fleet, cross the stile into the field on the left and follow this path which follows a line close to the shore before reaching a wooden bridge. Join the track and turn left then right upon reaching the village keeping to the lane back to the pub.

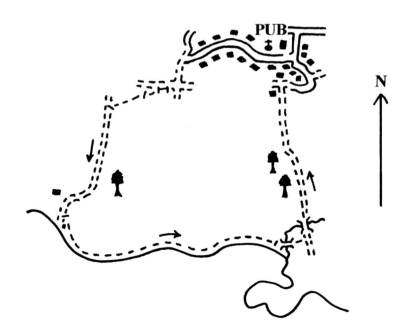

The Pilot Boat Inn, Lyme Regis

Historic Lyme Regis is located on the coast, west of the county on the A3052.

The Pilot Boat Inn lies in Bridge Street in a lovely position just back from the sea-front overlooking Cobb Gate Beach. There is a comfortably furnished sunny front bar with more tables at the rear. Recommended in many guides the pub is open all day serving very good food from 12 noon–10. Families are welcome. There is a small short stay car park close to the rear of the pub with much more room in the Charmouth Road car park a short way up the main A3052 approach road.

Approximate distance: 2½ miles. OS maps Landranger 193 & Explorer 116. Reference 344/922.

Close to the Devon border nestling in a sheltered vale lies the timeless seaside town of Lyme Regis, its famous Cobb featuring in the film of John Fowles novel, The French Lieutenant's Woman. The area is rich in fossils, evidence of which can be seen in the many town centre shops and museums. Sir George Somers, who discovered the Bermudas was born here as was Arthur Gregory who showed Queen Elizabeth's spies how to open letters without breaking the seal. Amongst its famous visitors were Jane Austen and Tennyson and the Duke of Monmouth once landed here with Daniel Defoe, the author of Robinson Crusoe.

This short but lovely scenic walk guides you first along the quay to the church then up the road to join a field path leading to Timber Hill. After negotiating an attractive rising path through a fine bluebell wood, a track and field path ultimately drops you down to the River Lim where a lovely riverside path leads you back to the town centre.

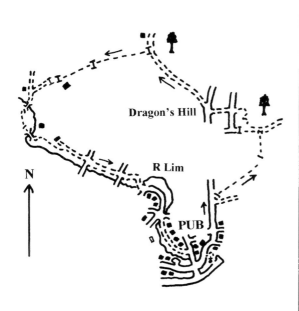

Walk No. 3

From the pub cross the road to the quay turning left through Gun Cliff Walk. Walk for a while then head left, up the steps to the church and out into the road turning right. Keeping to the right-hand side carefully walk up the hill and just beyond the car park look for the stile on the right. Bearing right walk up and across the field maintaining direction over a stile and through a couple of kissing gates before reaching the track at the top.

Turn left, and just before reaching the gate take the signposted coast path on the right. Keep to this attractive twisting path which rises through a delightful bluebell wood bearing left a short distance up onto a smaller undulating path which twists to the left then drops down to the lane. Cross to the narrow signed path opposite, turning right into the road at the bottom.

Broad Street

Join the bridleway opposite, signposted Penn 2¾. Pass through the caravan park and onto the track. Ignore the first signed footpath on the left but continue down until you reach the bridleway on the left (Liberty Trail). Pass through the gate and head down the field, through a similar gate making for a gate at the bottom. Continue down between the trees turning left just before the dwelling onto the signposted bridleway. Go over the bridge turning left and cross the field to the bridge on the far side after which keep to the

drive or follow the permissive path close to the river; the banks of which are lined in early spring with masses of garlic smelling ransoms.

Cross the road into Windsor Terrace and further on into Jericho keeping to the path past the cottages to the bridge. For added interest turn right onto the Riverside Path leading to Town Mill which passes the Leper's Well. Back out in the street turn right then finally right again along the narrow back streets, lined with interesting shops and small cafes.

View of the Cobb from Timber Hill

Cobb Gate Beach

River Lim

The Smugglers Inn, Osmington Mills

Osmington Mills is signed from the A353 east of Weymouth.

The pretty 13th century, stone and cob thatched Smugglers Inn, occupies an idyllic spot beside a stream just yards from the sea. Extended over the years the inn provides ample accommodation for drinkers and diners alike. There are 6 en-suite bedrooms. Summer time opening is all day from 11–11, Sunday 12 noon. Families welcome. There is a car park on the cliff opposite.

Approximate distance: 3 miles. OS maps: Landranger 194 & Outdoor Leisure 15. Reference 735/817.

The area has inspired many, not least Constable, who spent his honeymoon here; it was from this spot that he painted his famous picture of Weymouth Bay.

A popular scenic, coastal walk the second part of which rises through a lush almost tropical wooded valley. Steep in a few places but generally good underfoot make it ideal walking for all the family.

Take the footpath at the side of the pub which passes beside old coastguard cottages leading to a stile. Cross the grass to a second stile climbing to the top of this undulating and often slippery section of the Dorset Coast Path. Looking back one has a good view of Weymouth and Portland Bill. Keep to the path, which dips gently towards the small seaside village of Ringstead. After descending the steps into Spring Bottom cross the little bridge and take the signed path on the left.

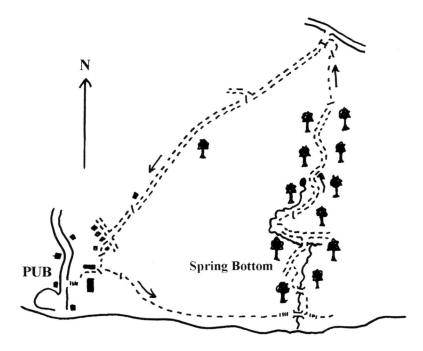

N

PUB

Spring Bottom

Further up bear left onto the narrow bridge crossing the stream and follow the little twisting path up through the copse to the track at the top turning right. At the fingerpost turn left and further on cross the stile bearing right to another stile beside a gate. The path beyond rises steadily through a lush green valley home to a wealth of wild-flowers and tropical looking plants.

A high avenue of trees line the route to the stile at the top. Keeping fairly close to the hedge go down the field to the stile at the bottom and almost immediately cross to the stile on the left then walk up the tarred drive. Climb the stile at the top and keep to the track beyond crossing a stile before descending to the drive.

Turn left and in a few steps join the signed path on the right, which drops down through the chalet park to a stile in the far hedge. Keep straight ahead rejoining the path back to the pub.

Ringstead Bay

The view west towards Weymouth

The Pulpit Inn, Portland

Portland is best reached from the A354 south of Dorchester.

The inn is situated at the southern most tip at the Bill of Portland. Accommodation is available in this friendly family pub where a holiday feel pervades. Present opening hours are 11.30–3 & 7–11.30. A carvery is served on Sunday. There is a large car park at the front of the pub also a public car park near the lighthouse.

Approximate distance: 5¼ miles. OS maps: Landranger 194 & Outdoor Leisure 15. Reference 677/687.

Portland is a migration stop for many birds over 300 species having been recorded, it is also home to 30 species of butterflies and some 720 species of moths. It is also famous for its Portland stone used in the construction of many major buildings including St Paul's Cathedral.

Wild flowers and butterflies abound all the way along this extremely enjoyable, scenic coastal walk which guides you, precariously in places, around the southern half of Portland. The route passes by the remains of St Andrew's Church, Avice Caro's cottage, the ruins of Rufus Castle - the oldest building on the Island and Pennsylvania Castle. The eastern side of the coast path can be a little demanding in places but negotiable with care. Try and walk in spring or summer preferably on a warm sunny day.

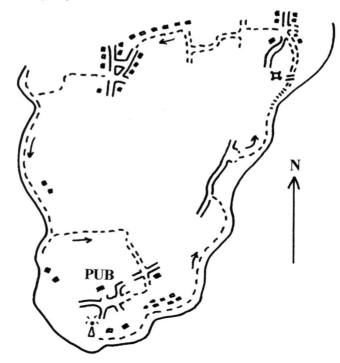

From the pub walk down to the lighthouse and turn left along the coast path passing at first between the beach huts. It is easy to follow needing little or no explanation and the scenery is stunning with numerous wild flowers and butterflies. Marbled whites and common blues can be seen flying around large swathes of red valerian which grows alongside blue viper's bugloss and yellow samphire. Undulating in places the path threads its way through several disused quarries before eventually rising to the road.

Turn right and a short distance later turn right again to the view point at Cheyne Weare. Picnic benches and information boards are provided. During spring and summer migrating birds can often be seen flying in the area. Continue north along the narrow coastal path, which although not hard to follow can be precarious in places. Try and keep to the path nearest to the cliff edge, where you will find some stone steps and the occasional yellow arrows to guide you. Upon reaching Church Ope Cove you can climb a short distance up the steps on the left if you wish to see the tombstones and derelict church. Otherwise continue up the steps on the right and follow the tarred drive under the arch, past the café and Avice Caro's cottage, (now a museum) and out to the road.

Turn right, cross over and join the signed footpath on the left beside the disused railway line. Turn left through the quarry then right passing round the gate and follow the track ahead. Further on turn right, walk up to the dwellings and turn left. Keep to the path behind the houses, which eventually reaches the Weston road.

Keep straight ahead beside the green, and almost opposite the turning on the left, cross the road and join the signed footpath opposite leading to the cliff edge. Wild flowers are everywhere along this particularly attractive path, which hugs the cliff top heading south. After passing the MOD buildings on the left take the path on the left signposted, East Cliff. Walk all around the edge of the field and down the track to the road turning right. After passing the field study centre take the path on the left then go right beside the quarry, a good place to observe birds and keep to the track past the dwellings back to the pub.

Quarry workings

The Anchor Inn, Seatown

Seatown, is signposted from the A35 at Chideock.

Duck Lane, narrow and single track in places eventually brings you to the coast where there is a car park opposite the inn (spaces limited at busy times). Situated yards from the beach this very popular family run pub serves very good food and ale every day of the week. Comfortable accommodation is available. Open all day in the summer the inn welcomes families.

Approximate distance: 3½ miles. OS maps: Landranger 193 and Explorer 29. Reference 420/918.

Golden Cap at 617 feet is the highest cliff on the south coast. Once aptly named, less of the golden sandstone is visible today due to the invasive growth of vegetation.

The first section of this lovely, scenic walk takes you up to and through Langdon Wood then down towards the coast across farmland and through an attractive wooded vale. After reaching ruined St Gabriel's chapel a strenuous climb brings you to the top of Golden Cap to be well rewarded by the breathtaking views during the descent to the Anchor Inn. The going is strenuous and although fairly firm underfoot can be wet and slippery during the winter. The best time is spring onwards especially when the bluebells are in bloom.

From the car park head a short distance back up the lane and join the signed footpath on the left. After a second stile bear slightly left across the field to the stile in the far hedge following the path up through the trees, over two more stiles and turn right.

The view east from Golden Cap

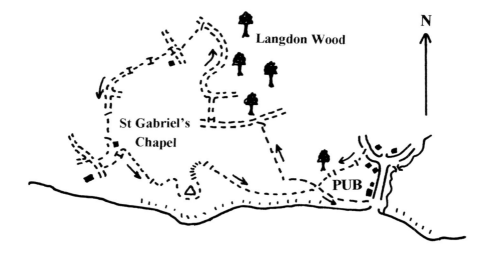

Part way up this steep and often slippery hillside bear right at the sign for Langdon Hill and walk up beside the boundary to the stile at the top.

Turn left onto the track, walk to the end then go through the gate on the right and up the narrow path through Langdon Wood turning left at the top. Follow this wide track through the woods where lots of bluebells and other wild flowers can be seen plus good views across Lyme Bay. Follow this undulating track looking for a stile on the left at which point go down the field to the gate, across the concrete farm road and through the gate into the field opposite (signposted St Gabriel's $\frac{1}{2}$).

Walk down the field, through the gate and continue to the gate at the bottom. A wild flower lined track lies beyond which drops down through a mature oak wood where bluebells and wild garlic ransoms flourish in abundance. Continue ahead at the bend and with the stream on your left, pass through the gate keeping close to the boundary and up to the fingerpost (can be very wet in winter). Go through the gate and along the track, through more gates before reaching the gravel drive at which point turn left.

Turn left by the dwelling making your way up to the ruined chapel of St Gabriel's. The cottages and ruined church are all that remain of the once thriving fishing village abandoned after the main road was re-routed in 1825. Carry on past the chapel, through the gate and turn right up the hillside making for the finger post at the top. The less energetic can follow the track ahead which bears right bringing you to the same spot. From the finger post head up the stepped path to the top of Golden Cap taking time to look back and enjoy the view. Go past the trig. point, down the steps to the kissing gate turning right to the stile. Stay on the coast path which drops down close to the beach back to the inn.

The Bankes Arms, Studland

Studland can be reached by road through Wareham but the best and most scenic route is to take the ferry from Sandbanks. Sailing every twenty minutes the first crossing is 7 am, the last 11 pm. Turn left in the village and then right following the signs for the Bankes Arms.

Owned by the National Trust this stone built inn occupies an enviable position overlooking Studland Bay. Conveniently open all day the inn offers good accommodation, and an interesting choice of food complimented by an excellent range of real ales. Families are welcome. Park in the National Trust car park.

Approximate distance of walk: 5½ miles. OS maps: Landranger 195 & Outdoor Leisure 15. Reference 036/828.

The Shell Bay peninsular and Studland are the property of The National Trust having been gifted the entire Bankes estate in 1981 by Mr Bankes following the death of Ralph Bankes. The whole area is a haven for wildlife.

This scenic walk starts at Studland and takes you round Handfast Point close to the famous Old Harry Rocks then high up onto Ballard Down. The return route is across Godlington Heath passing beside the impressive Agglestone followed by a series of field paths. Generally good underfoot the walk is very hilly in places and a bit demanding but the scenery is stunning.

Turn right from the pub walking downhill until you reach the path by the toilet block signposted, to Old Harry.

The path leads directly to Old Harry Rocks. Just before reaching Handfast Point there is a small wood, which is

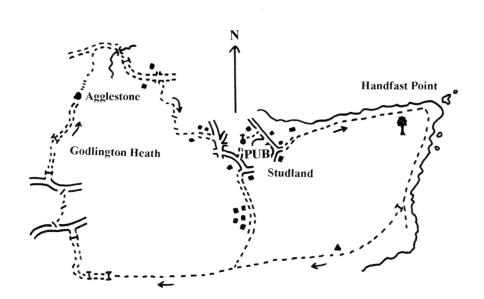

open to the public and home to vast areas of garlic ransoms. Round the point and continue westwards up the down then pass through the small wooden gate on the right following the bridleway up and over the rise. After passing the trig. point keep straight ahead along the ridge enjoying views both over Poole Harbour and Swanage Bay. For a short walk a path is signposted by the large stone block on the right which will take you straight back to the village. Continue ahead eventually reaching a gate and track beyond which passes beside the obelisk, removed in 1941 it was re-erected several years after the war by the men of 129 Field Squadron. Carry on following the track round and down to the right to meet the road.

Turn left crossing to the opposite verge walking until you reach the stile and signposted path on the right. Bearing right walk up the field to the stile, through the narrow bluebell wood and carefully across the golf course to the stile. Turn left into the lane and almost immediately join the signed bridleway on the right entering Godlington

Heath. The path is fairly straightforward at first crossing the golf course. Fork left at the marker stone and continue along the path in the direction of the Agglestone which soon looms large in the distance. Walk up to and round the stone, down the stepped path on the far side following it as it twists its way over the heath before reaching a sandy track at which point turn right.

Further on cross the small wooden bridge, pass through the gate and follow the track until you come to a signed footpath on the right. It runs beside the bridleway eventually joining with it. Keep straight ahead and look for a stile on the left, cross the field to the stile opposite and turn left along the narrow path which soon merges with the drive to the dwellings before reaching the road.

Turn right and go up the hill then take the second left by The Studland Stores into School Lane. Walk round and down very soon to reach a signed path on the left, which passes beside the church, and carries on behind bringing you out beside the car park.

The Agglestone

The Pinnacles

Old Harry

The Bankes Arms

Bridport Arms Hotel, West Bay

West Bay is signed from the A35 Bridport by-pass.

Attractively thatched the inn occupies an enviable position on the edge of the shingle beach with seats overlooking the harbour. The lounge is on two levels providing comfortable areas for both dining and drinking. Conveniently open every day, all day the inn welcomes families and can offer overnight accommodation. There is parking beside the wall opposite the pub, ample pay and display car parks close by, on the approach road and at the old station yard car park.

Approximate distance: 4¼ miles. OS maps: Landranger 193 & Outdoor Leisure 15. Reference 463/904.

West Bay is a popular holiday resort with an attractive harbour. This extremely enjoyable walk at first guides you along the course of the old railway then up a pretty bridlepath onto Bothenhampton Nature Reserve. Further paths lead you to Bridport before returning along a lovely path beside the River Brit.

Walk back to the road and turn right past the shops crossing over when you reach the old railway car park. Carry on past the station following the course of the old railway, which eventually reaches the B3157. Cross over and join the signed bridleway opposite. This very attractive, primrose lined path winds its way steadily to the lane at the top. Keep straight ahead past the dwellings and through the gate onto Bothenhampton Nature Reserve. A short way in take the small path downhill on the left and either fork left over the crossing point which passes the old lime kiln or carry on ahead. Leave by the gate at the bottom, follow the track up to the road, turn right and join the signed footpath on the left.

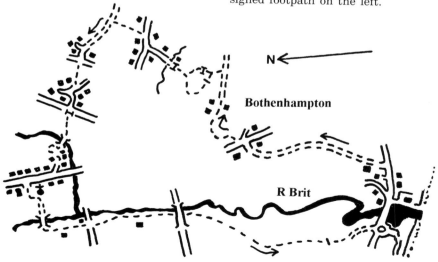

N ←

Bothenhampton

R Brit

The harbour at West Bay

This very attractive, deeply cut, stone sided gully rises steadily to a track at which point turn left, enter the cul-de-sac and, keeping to the pavement on the left walk down to the road and cross to the footpath opposite signposted, Bridport ¾. Pass between the dwellings at the bottom carefully crossing the by-pass to the kissing gate opposite.

Keep straight ahead, cross the river and join the path behind the houses round to the gate, up the lane turning right into the road. Cross over and walk up to St Mary's church, past the front entrance and take the path on the left round behind the church and join the tarred path leading to the River Brit. Go over the bridge and turn left along this very attractive riverside path. Cross the road and continue ahead on the signed footpath. Bear left past the thatched dwelling, through the kissing gate keeping to the path under the by-pass. Well signed the path bears right to a gate, follows the length of the fields through a couple more gates before reaching the caravan park. Bear left along the path and up to the road walking back round the harbour to the pub.

The Manor Hotel, West Bexington

Village signed from the B3157, Bridport to Abbotsbury road at Swyre.

West Bexington is a small hamlet comprising a few dwellings, a farm and the Manor Hotel. Situated beneath the main building the very cosy and atmospheric bar is heated by an open fire. There is also a light and airy conservatory for family dining. Accommodation is available. Hours are all day every day with excellent food served 12–2 and from 7–10. Park at the hotel or in the public car park on Chesil Beach.

Approximate distance: 3 miles. OS maps: Landranger 193 & Outdoor Leisure 15. Reference 533/866.

A little demanding this often-bracing walk follows the Dorset Coast Path along the pebble beach before climbing up Tulk's and Limekiln Hills finally descending on an attractive track.

Walk down to the beach and turn left along the shingle covered path walking for just over a mile until you reach the marker stone and gated footpath on the left signed Hillfort 1½. Climb up the track to the gate and continue ahead on this gently rising grass track keeping straight ahead across the farm entrance bearing left onto the track behind the barn leading to a gate. Bear half right across the field making for the stile in the hedge opposite then turn immediately right up the field to the stile at the top.

At the fingerpost turn left keeping to the path up the hillside, past the barn and on to the track ahead rising fairly steeply before reaching open pasture. Maintain direction to the stone stile whilst enjoying the distant view of Golden Cap. Further ahead the path drops down past the old limekiln before reaching a stile. Cross the lay-by to the track opposite following it downhill through sheep gates, beside a newly rebuilt dry stone wall eventually reaching the lane back to the pub.

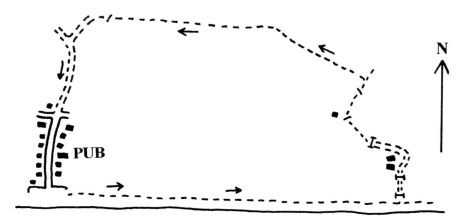

The Manor Hotel

Re-built dry stone walling

The Square & Compass, Worth Matravers

The pretty Purbeck village of Worth Matravers is signed from the B3069, Corfe Castle to Swanage road between Kingston and Langton Matravers. National Trust car park on the right just before reaching the village.

The lovely Square & Compass has long been one of my favourite pubs. It is totally original and the most unspoilt pub in Dorset if not in England. A narrow stone passage leads to the small servery where real ale is still served traditionally straight from the cask. Heated by an open log fire the small lounge has a wealth of paraphernalia. There is a cosy snug, a fossil museum and rear beer garden. Chickens scratch amongst the old implements and tools strewn around at the front where rustic benches are ideally positioned to enjoy the sunny sea view. Opposite the pub is the Worth Cafe and Craft Centre.   Hours 11.30–3 and 6–11.

Approximate distance: 4 miles. OS maps: Landranger 195 & Outdoor Leisure 15. Reference 974/775.

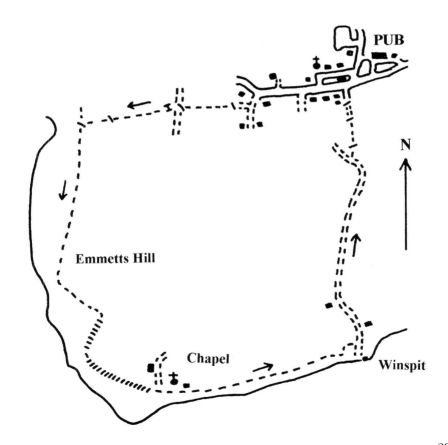

Walk No. 10

Tranquil Worth Matravers was for many years the centre for the quarrying of Purbeck marble its attractive stone built cottages clustered around the small village pond and green.

This very scenic and often bracing walk is moderately strenuous but generally good underfoot. Level walking takes you to the top of Emmetts Hill beyond which are two demanding flights of steps before arriving at the top of St Aldhelm's Head. At 354 feet above sea level the only buildings are old coastguard cottages, a shore watch lookout and an 800-year-old chapel. After a gradual descent to the now abandoned Winspit quarries a track rises steadily back to the village.

From the car park walk down towards the village bearing right past the duck pond and up the lane walking towards Weston Farm where a path on the left is signposted St Aldhelm's Head 1½. Take the signposted path off the track to the right and cross the stile into the field. On the far side climb the stile, cross the track and pass through the gate following the sign to Chapman's Pool. A couple of stiles later turn left and join the Dorset Coast Path walking along the ridge.

A steep descent down Emmetts Hill is followed by an even steeper and longer climb up to the top of St Aldhelm's Head. The chapel dedicated to St Aldhelm was built in the 12th cen-

tury and has long acted as a mark for seafarers. Continue along the coast path and after passing some derelict cottages take the right fork, following the path, which descends gently towards Winspit.

Wild cabbage can be found in abundance and you may be lucky to spot the occasional early spider orchid, emblem for the Dorset Trust for Nature Conservation. Upon reaching the track head inland and near the top fork right by the marker stone indicating ½ to Worth. Cross the stile into the field and keep straight ahead up and over the rise to the stile then simply follow the path ahead back past the pond to the car park.

Emmetts Hill

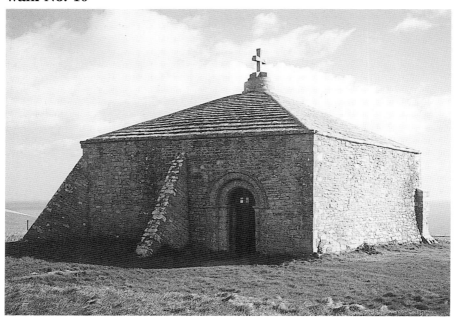

St. Aldhelm's Chapel

Abandoned stone quarries at Winspit